101
TALKS
FOR
CHILDREN

MARIANNE J. SHAMPTON

101
TALKS
FOR
CHILDREN

READY-TO-LEARN TALKS WITH A GUIDE FOR HELPING CHILDREN PREPARE TALKS

BOOKCRAFT
SALT LAKE CITY, UTAH

Library of Congress Catalog Card Number: 85-73025
ISBN: 0-88494-580-4

10th Printing, 1993

Printed in the United States of America

Preface

Sometimes children think that the scriptures are for adults only or that the scriptures are too difficult to understand. But children need to use the scriptures from the very start. Christ said: "Man shall not live by bread alone, but by every word that proceedeth out of the mouth of God" (Matthew 4:4). If children grow up with the scriptures, the scriptures will not seem strange or difficult to them.

I hope that this book will promote a kind of talk rarely used by children—a talk that uses scriptures—and that this will lead to a new understanding of the scriptures for children.

Contents

7

9

10

Hints for Parents

Parents need to teach a child how to prepare and how to give talks. If taught from the time he enters Primary, a child can learn how to give a well-prepared, well-delivered talk.

Preparing the Talk

1. Pray with your child. Ask Heavenly Father for his help. He will guide you in choosing a subject, in finding material, and in organizing it. Through prayer, a child will learn he is not alone; he has his parents and the Lord to help him.

2. With your child, choose a topic to speak on. It should be one he can understand. A four-year-old, for example, might understand something of prayer, the importance of reverence while in the Lord's house, and the need to obey one's parents. A seven-year-old might have some understanding of repentance, baptism, and the sacrament. Clearly, the subject of a talk should fit a child's age.

3. Help your child develop the skill to speak without reading his talk. For very small children, parents will obviously need to write a short talk for the child, with the child learning it by heart. A child not able to read could hold pictures or a small notecard with pictures on it to remind him of what to say (see the talk "Primary" for an example). A parent should also be prepared to prompt a small child if needed.

Later, perhaps around the age of ten, the child might be able to put his own words together, possibly by having a three-by-five card in front of him containing a scripture and a word or two for each subtopic to remind him. A short outline is preferable to a talk written out word for word.

One excellent way for a child to remember his talk is to base the talk on a gospel or scriptural story. This allows the child to tell a familiar story and teach a gospel principle while doing so. And stories are often easier to remember than even simple outlines of gospel subjects.

4. A talk usually has three parts: a beginning (the introduction), a middle (the development), and an end (the conclusion).

   A. The beginning: One possible way to begin a talk is with a scripture. Read several pertinent scriptures with your child and allow him to choose the one he will use. Then help him prepare a short explanation of the scripture, introducing the topic of his talk. For example, in a talk on baptism, a child might read or recite Matthew 3:16: "And Jesus, when he was baptized, went up straightway out of the water"—going on to say, "When we turn eight, we must also be baptized as Jesus was."

   B. The middle: Bring in material that supports the child's topic. Ask your child how he feels about the subject and write—or have him write—his feelings. As much as possible, use the child's personal experiences in his talk, or at least the experiences of parents, brothers, sisters, relatives, or friends. The child can easily tell such stories and will feel comfortable with them. For short talks, do not complicate the child's talk with additional scriptures or with poems.

   C. The end: Usually conclude a talk by summing up the main points covered. Repeat, perhaps, the opening scripture. Have the child bear a short testimony (if appropriate), and then close in the name of Jesus Christ.

Preparing the Child to Give His Talk

After your child has prepared his talk, help him get ready to give it. If he knows what is expected of him, what he's going to say, and where he will be, you will have helped him overcome any fear.

1. Have your child practice saying his talk out loud. Help him to correctly pronounce every word in the scripture he has chosen. If the talk is a week or more away, have the child give his talk in family home evening so that he might get accustomed to speaking in front of people. If your ward or branch meetings are in a late morning or in an afternoon block, the child might practice giving his talk in front of his family before going to church.

In regular family home evenings, have each child take turns giving talks. That way, he will be more likely to have talks prepared for church, and he will become used to speaking in public. He will also have more confidence.

2. Tell your child to stand straight and tall. Remind him not to lean on the pulpit.

3. Have your child talk clearly and slowly, so he can be understood. If the people in the audience can hear and understand the person speaking, they will listen and be more reverent.

4. Tell the child that people will look at him as he speaks, but that they are his friends. He does not need to be frightened.

5. If he is very young, tell the child where to stand (at the pulpit).

6. The day of the talk is very important. Pray with the child so he can feel calm and know he has the support of his parents and his Heavenly Father.

7. Arrive early so the child can be in his seat before the meeting starts.

8. Tell the child to take a deep breath before beginning and to smile. Tell him to be calm and remind him that he is prepared. Perhaps read Doctrine and Covenants 38:30: "If ye are prepared ye shall not fear."

If parents go through these steps with a child, he will soon learn how to speak in public. Eventually, he will be able to give a good talk by himself (with the Lord's help, of course).

1

Stories from the Scriptures

The Creation

God made this beautiful world for us to live on. It took six days. The Bible tells us what he made first:

On the first day, he made the day and the night.
On the second day, he divided the waters.
On the third day, he made dry land appear with trees and flowers.
On the fourth day, he made the sun, the moon, and the stars.
On the fifth day, he made the birds and the fish.
On the sixth day, he made the rest of the animals, and then he made man.
On the seventh day, he rested.

Genesis 1:31 reads: "And God saw every thing that he had made, and, behold, it was very good." In our prayers, we should thank Heavenly Father for all the wonderful things he made for us.

Daniel

Daniel was a good man. We can read about him in the Bible. He prayed to Heavenly Father every day.

There were some bad men who did not like Daniel. They helped pass a law so Daniel could not pray. Then the men watched Daniel. When he said his prayers, he was arrested and put in the lion's den.

The Lord protected Daniel. He shut the lions' mouths so they could not hurt Daniel. The next day Daniel was let out unharmed.

Just as God protected and watched over Daniel, he will watch over us.

David and Goliath

Goliath was a giant and a very mean man. He wanted the Israelites to be slaves to his people.

There was to be a final battle. If Goliath won, the Israelites would be slaves. If Goliath lost, the Israelites would be free. Because Goliath was so big, no one would fight him.

A young man named David offered to fight. He loved his country and knew God would help him win. The king offered David his armor, but David was too small to wear it. Instead, he took only his slingshot and three small stones.

Goliath laughed when he saw David. He thought it was a joke. He soon stopped laughing. David said: "Thou comest to me with a sword, and with a spear, and with a shield: but I come to thee in the name of the Lord of hosts, the God of the armies of Israel, whom thou hast defied" (Samuel 17:45). David put a stone in his slingshot, aimed, and hit Goliath's head; Goliath fell dead.

Because David loved Israel and had faith in God, he was able to kill his enemy. God did not want the Israelites to be slaves, he wanted them to be free.

Like David, we should have faith in God.

The Good Samaritan

Once a man asked Jesus who his neighbor was, Jesus told the following parable or story.

There was a man walking on the road going to the town of Jericho. Some thieves came, beat the man up, and took his money. They left him wounded and dying on the side of the road.

A priest was walking on the same road. When he saw the hurt man, he crossed to the other side of the road.

A Levite came and did the same thing. Neither man would help the poor stranger.

Another man, a Samaritan, came down the road. He saw the hurt man. He knelt down beside him and took care of his wounds. He put the man on his donkey and took him into town. He left him with an innkeeper and gave him money to pay for the sick man's needs.

The last man, the Samaritan, was truly a good neighbor. He helped the injured man even though he didn't know him.

We are all each other's neighbors. We should be kind to everyone and help those we meet.

Jesus Fed Five Thousand

Once Jesus left the city and went to the desert. When the people heard where Jesus was, they followed him. They wanted his blessings.

Jesus felt sorry for the people so he blessed them. It was getting late. There were so many people. Because they were in the desert, there was nothing to eat. All they had were five loaves of bread and two fish. Jesus took the bread and fish. He broke it and blessed it. All the people ate and were filled. No one was hungry. Five thousand men plus women and children had eaten.

With Jesus all things are possible. If God wishes, he can do anything. We should remember this story and remember that God can help us with all of our problems.

Jesus Helps Others

When Jesus was on the earth he did many miracles. He raised the dead; he calmed the sea; he fed thousands; he walked on water. He made the blind to see, the deaf to hear. He healed the sick.

Jesus was always thinking of others. He tried to help those in need. The last time he ate with his disciples he washed their feet. Even when he was on the cross he said: "Father, forgive them; for they know not what they do" (Luke 23:34). He was not thinking of himself, only of others.

We should try to be like Jesus. We should help others. I hope we will think of others and not ourselves.

Jesus' Second Coming

Jesus told a story about ten women who were waiting for a bridegroom to come. All ten women had lamps to use during the wedding feast, but only five had enough oil. The five that were not prepared with enough oil had to leave to find some more. While they were gone the bridegroom came, and the five women missed him.

Jesus was trying to tell us to prepare for his second coming. The things we do are like oil in our lamps. Going to church, paying our tithing, saying our prayers, and speaking well of others are all things we can do.

Doctrine and Covenants 38:30 tell us: "If ye are prepared ye shall not fear." I hope we will start preparing today for when Jesus comes again.

Jesus Was Tempted

One day Jesus went into the wilderness. He had been fasting for forty days. He was fasting to prepare for his mission and to get closer to Heavenly Father.

Satan appeared to Jesus and tried to tempt him. He told Jesus to turn the rocks into bread so he could eat. Jesus said he would only use his power to help others.

Satan told Jesus to jump off a high place and let the angels catch him. Jesus said he would not test his Father.

Satan wanted Jesus to worship and obey him. Jesus told Satan he would only obey God; then he commanded Satan to leave.

When we are tempted to do wrong, we should remember this story and choose the right. We should think, "What would Jesus want me to do?"

Job

In the Bible there is a book about a very righteous man. It is the book of Job.

Job loved the Lord and praised him. Satan tried to tempt Job to turn him against the Lord. He caused Job to lose his family and property; Job was covered with boils all over his body and was in a lot of pain.

Job's friends told him he was being punished for something he had done. Job knew this was not true. He endured to the end. Job said: "But [God] knoweth the way that I take: when he hath tried me, I shall come forth as gold" (Job 23:10).

We all have problems. We all get sick. Everything isn't perfect all the time. But we can learn from our problems. We came to earth to gain experience. Pain, sickness, and unhappiness are all part of life.

The opposite of hot is cold. The opposite of day is night. The opposite of sickness is health. We have to know one to know the other.

I hope we can learn from our problems and not complain about them. I hope that, like Job, we can come forth as gold after passing through our problems.

Jonah and the Fish

Long ago there was a man named Jonah. The Lord told Jonah to go to the city of Nineveh. It was a wicked city, and the people were very bad. If they did not repent, the city would be destroyed.

Jonah was afraid to go to Nineveh, so he ran from God. He got on a boat and sailed away. This made God unhappy, so he caused a great storm on the sea. The boat was tossed to and fro. The sailors were afraid they would drown. They woke up Jonah from his sleep. They asked him who he was and what he had done to displease his God. Then they threw him into the sea.

The Lord caused a big fish to swallow Jonah. While in the fish's belly, Jonah prayed for forgiveness. God forgave Jonah and made the fish spit Jonah out.

Jonah went to the city of Nineveh and told the people to repent. They all did. The king made a law for all in the city to fast. They dressed in sackcloth to show God they were sorry. They prayed for forgiveness. Because of this the city was saved and not destroyed.

We should always do what God asks us to do. We cannot hide from him. He always knows where we are, what we are doing, and what we are thinking.

Liahona

Lehi was a very good man. He lived in Jerusalem. He told the people to repent, but they would not. The Lord told Lehi to take his family out of Jerusalem and go into the wilderness. He would lead them to the promised land.

One morning when Lehi got up he found a round, brass ball with two arrows on it sitting in front of his tent. This instrument was called the Liahona. God gave it to Lehi to direct his family. It worked by faith. If they had faith and were obeying the commandments the arrow would show them where to go. Sometimes words would appear on the ball. These words gave counsel to the people.

There are many stories about the Liahona. I would like to tell you one. Once Nephi broke his bow. There was nothing to eat and everyone was getting very hungry. Nephi made a new bow. He prayed that Heavenly Father would help him find some food. He took the Liahona with him. Because he prayed and showed he had faith, the Liahona pointed the way for Nephi. He found some food, and all were grateful.

The Liahona was passed down from generation to generation. The last time it was seen was by Joseph Smith and the three witnesses.

We don't have a Liahona, but if we have faith and do what is right the Lord will still direct us.

Noah

In the Bible we find the story about a man named Noah. He was a prophet. He told the people to repent, but they laughed at him. In the whole world, Noah and his family were the only people obeying God.

God told Noah to build an ark, which is a big boat. He told Noah how to make it and what kind of wood to use. While Noah built the ark, other people laughed at him.

God told Noah to put two of every kind of animal on the ark. He gathered pigs and horses and cows and sheep. He found birds and monkeys and tigers and hippopotamuses. He got tiny bees and huge elephants. Two of every kind.

Noah also put food and seeds in the ark. Then he took his wife and sons and their wives into the ark and shut the door. The people were still laughing.

Then it started to rain. It rained and rained and rained. The bad people stopped laughing, but it was too late. It rained for forty days and forty nights. Soon the whole earth was covered with water. Noah and his family lived in the ark and took care of the animals.

When the rain stopped and dry land finally appeared, Noah and his family came out of the ark and built an altar. They thanked Heavenly Father for saving them.

God created a rainbow and made it appear in the sky. He promised Noah that he would never flood the whole earth again. The rainbow still reminds us of God's promise.

When a prophet says something will happen, it does happen. We should do what the prophets tell us to do.

Parable of the Sower

Jesus told a story about a sower, someone who plants seeds. In the story, some of the seeds fall by the side and the birds eat the seeds. Some of the seeds fall on stony ground. They grow fast but the sun burns them up so they wither away. Some seeds fall among the thorns and the thorns choke out the fruit. The last seeds go into good soil. They grow and increase and yield good fruit.

The people did not understand all of Jesus' story. They wanted to know how it applied to them. Jesus explained:

The sower is the word of God or the gospel.

Some words fall by the wayside and Satan takes them away so they can not be heard.

The words that fall on stony ground are like people who hear the word and receive it but cannot endure the persecution.

The words among the thorns are like people who choose worldly riches rather than God.

The last words in good soil are like good people who hear the gospel, accept it, are baptized, and then teach it. Just as the fruits increase, the gospel increases by our missionary work.

I hope we can all be like the good soil and let the gospel grow.

Scriptures

Matthew 4:4 reads: "Man shall not live by bread alone, but by every word that proceedeth out of the mouth of God." God's words are in the scriptures. The scriptures include the Bible, the Book of Mormon, the Doctrine and Covenants, and the Pearl of Great Price. These books tell about God and God's people from the very beginning.

The Bible tells us about the creation of the world; Noah and the ark; David and Goliath; and Christ's birth, life, and death. The Book of Mormon is about the people here on the American continents. The Doctrine and Covenants and the Pearl of Great Price are largely God's words to the people of his church today.

The scriptures teach us what is right. They can help us solve our problems. They can also help us stay close to the Lord. Our prophet has told us that we should read the scriptures every day. I hope we will all try to read the scriptures.

Shadrach, Meshach, and Abed-nego

The Bible tells us about a king named Nebuchadnezzar. This king made a golden image and commanded everyone to worship it.

There were three young men who would not worship the image. Their names were Shadrach, Meshach, and Abed-nego. The king told them that he would put them in a fire and burn them if they did not worship the idol. They told the king that they would only pray to their God, our Heavenly Father.

The king was angry. He had the furnace made seven times hotter than normal. The guards that put them into the fire were burned because it was so hot.

The king was astonished at what happened next. He saw four persons, not just three, in the fire. An angel had come to protect the three young men. They were not harmed by the fire.

The king let them out and said that they were blessed. Then he made a law to protect them.

We should remember Shadrach, Meshach, and Abed-nego. They had courage and faith. We should have that same courage and faith. God will help us if we keep his commandments.

Ten Lepers

When Jesus was alive there was no cure for a terrible disease called leprosy. When people got sick with leprosy, they had to leave their families and go live alone in the desert so they would not spread the disease to others. These people were called lepers.

One day when Jesus was walking to another city, ten lepers called to him. They had heard stories of his miracles, and they believed Jesus could make them better. They said: "Jesus, Master, have mercy on us" (Luke 17:13). Jesus told them to go show themselves to their priest and they would be healed. Only one of the ten lepers went back to thank Jesus for this miracle.

We should be like that man. We should give the Lord thanks for all he does for us. We need to be thankful for all our blessings.

The Tower of Babel

When the earth was first created all the people spoke the same language. Everyone could understand each other.

They decided to build a city and a tower that would reach to heaven. The tower got taller and taller. The people were proud and boastful of the tower.

The Lord did not like this. People cannot get to heaven or close to God by building a tower. He confused their language. They couldn't work together because they couldn't understand each other. They were scattered over the earth.

We should remember that the way to get to heaven is through prayer, obeying the commandments, and reading the scriptures. I hope we will all try the right way to get closer to our Heavenly Father.

Two Thousand Stripling Warriors

In the Book of Mormon is a story about a town that had a lot of faith. The people of the town buried their weapons and promised God they would never fight again. Everything was fine for a while, and the people were happy.

Then times changed. Bad people wanted to take over the town and not let the good people worship God. The people were afraid for their lives and their freedom, so they thought about breaking their promise. Helaman, one of the men in charge, told the people that they should keep their promise to God.

The sons of these people said that only the parents had made the promise, not them. They had been taught faith by their mothers. They believed God would protect them.

Helaman took these two thousand young men. They had never fought before. They didn't know how, but the Lord was with them. The battle was horrible, and many warriors were killed and wounded. When it was over they found that many of Helaman's young men were hurt or wounded but not one was killed. They had won the fight.

The town was happy and excited. They were glad they had kept their promise to Heavenly Father.

We should always keep our promises. If we promise our moms and dads, our friends, our teachers, or Heavenly Father, we should keep the promise no matter what. A promise is a promise.

When Jesus Was Twelve

When Jesus was twelve years old, his parents thought that he was lost. They looked all over for three days but couldn't find him.

When they finally found Jesus, he was teaching the men in the temple. "And all that heard him were astonished at his understanding and answers" (Luke 2:47). He told his mother that he was doing his Heavenly Father's business.

Even though Jesus was just twelve years old, he knew enough about the gospel to teach grown men about it. We should also try to learn as much as we can so that if someone asks us about the Church, we can give a good answer.

Women in the Scriptures

We hear a lot of stories about men in the scriptures and their courage and faithfulness. Sometimes we forget the special women who are mentioned in the scriptures.

Eve was the first woman on earth. We are all descended from her. Moses' mother saved his life by hiding him in the river. Mary was the mother of Jesus. She was blessed above all women. Luke 1:30 tells us: "And the angel said unto her, Fear not, Mary: for thou hast found favor with God." Sarah, the wife of Abraham, had faith in God and gave birth to a son when she was very old. Even the Book of Mormon tells of the two thousand stripling warriors whose lives were saved because their mothers had taught them to have faith.

Both men and women are very important in the scriptures.

2

Gospel Teachings

Fasting

The first Sunday of every month, we are asked to fast and give to the Church the money we would have spent on food. These are called *fast offerings,* and the money is used to buy needed things for the poor.

When we fast, we should be happy and not complain. We should not look sad or grumpy. The Lord knows we are fasting, and no one else needs to know. Jesus said: "When ye fast, be not, as the hypocrites, of a sad countenance: for they disfigure their faces, that they may appear unto men to fast. Verily I say unto you, They have their reward." (Matthew 6:16.)

We are promised that the Lord will bless us if we fast. We should all try to fast as Jesus wants us to.

Food Makes a Difference

Daniel was a prophet in the Old Testament. Daniel knew good food was important. He and his friends had to live with the king's men and eat the king's food. The king ate meat and drank wine.

Daniel knew he should not eat the king's food. He made a deal that he and his friends would eat "pulse" and drink water. Pulse is made of dried seeds, peas, and beans. After ten days they would see who was the healthiest, Daniel or the king's men.

Daniel won. For the next three years he and his friends ate the pulse and water. The king was delighted at the results; all were healthy and wise. The Lord blessed them for eating good food.

If we eat good food like fruits and vegetables and drink lots of water and milk, we will be healthy.

God's Colorful Creations

When I look at my paints and see the different colors, it reminds me of the beautiful things in the world that God created.

Red is for roses, hearts, and big juicy apples.
Yellow is for lemons, daffodils, and the bright sun-
shine.
Blue is for water, blue jays, and the cloudless sky.
Green is for leaves, grass, and great big watermelons.
Orange is for pumpkins, squash, and goldfish.
Purple is for grapes, plums, and little pansies.

When I mix the colors together, they remind me of Heavenly Father's most beautiful creations, like sunsets, rainbows, and butterflies.

I'm glad this world is so full of such beautiful colors.

Note: The child might hold up a piece of colored paper as he talks about each color.

How Prayers Are Answered

The Lord does answer our prayers, but we have to do our part too. We can't just ask and expect him to do everything.

We should follow four steps to pray:

1. We should think about our problem and the different ways we could solve it.
2. We should choose the best solution.
3. We should pray and ask God if we chose the right solution.
4. We should listen for the answer.

If we feel good inside, we know our decision is right. If we feel confused and uneasy, the choice is wrong. Then we need to go back to step number one again.

I hope we remember these four steps when we pray.

Jesus Loves Little Children

I am a child of God. I know Heavenly Father and Jesus love me. I am important to them.

The Bible tells a story about when Jesus was very tired, but he still let the mothers bring their children to him. He held and blessed the children.

The Book of Mormon tells of when Jesus was resurrected and came to America. He blessed the people. Then he took the children into a circle and angels from heaven circled them and blessed them.

Jesus said that we must become like little children if we want to get to heaven.

I am glad Jesus loves little children. I hope we can make him proud of us by the things we do and say.

Miracles

When Jesus was on earth he performed many miracles. He made the blind see and the lame walk. He healed the sick, fed large crowds, and even raised the dead.

The scriptures tell us we must have faith before there can be a miracle. We must believe. The prophet Ether said: "For if there be no faith among the children of men God can do no miracle among them" (Ether 12:12).

Even today there are miracles. Many people are made well after being sick when they have faith and are given a priesthood blessing. People close to death are sometimes healed. We must believe in miracles and in the priesthood today.

Missionary Work

When the Church was being restored, the Lord said: "A great and marvelous work is about to come forth unto the children of men" (D&C 14:1). This great and marvelous work is missionary work. We should all be missionaries. Every member of the Church is a missionary. Every young man nineteen years old should go on a mission. Young women can go on missions too. We can prepare for our missions now. We can learn the gospel, learn to cook and clean, and learn to save our money so that we will have enough to go on our missions.

We can also be missionaries now. We can invite our friends to come to Primary with us. We can invite them to family home evening. We can set a good example and do what is right. We can let them see how happy we are as members of The Church of Jesus Christ of Latter-day Saints.

I hope we will all be good missionaries.

39

Music

The Lord said: "The song of the righteous is a prayer unto me, and it shall be answered with a blessing upon their heads" (D&C 25:12).

Music is very important. Jesus and his disciples sang a hymn before they went to Gethsemane to pray. When the Church was first organized, the Lord called Emma Smith to select songs for a hymn book. The pioneers sang songs around the campfire to praise God, and singing helped ease their burdens. We sing a sacrament hymn about Jesus before we take the sacrament to put us in the right spirit and to help us think of him.

The songs we sing in Primary were written by inspiration and help us praise the Lord and learn more about his church. Most of the songs teach gospel principles. We should all enjoy singing and try to learn all the words to the songs we sing.

My Body Is a Temple

We sing a song in Primary called "My Body Is a Temple." Our bodies are the temples or houses for our spirits. 1 Corinthians 3:16 reads: "Know ye not that ye are the temple of God, and that the Spirit of God dwelleth in you?"

Because our bodies are where our spirits dwell, we should keep our bodies clean, our spirits clean, and our minds clean. We should put only good foods into our bodies. We should also put only good thoughts into our minds.

41

We are promised in the Word of Wisdom that we will be blessed if we are obedient and we keep ourselves clean inside and out. I hope we can all remember that our bodies are temples for our spirits.

Organization of the True Church

The sixth article of faith reads: "We believe in the same organization that existed in the Primitive Church, namely, apostles, prophets, pastors, teachers, evangelists, and so forth.

When we study the Bible we find out how Christ organized his church. We learn about the offices and teachings of his church. We know it was organized correctly because Christ did it himself.

Some of the things Jesus taught were: baptism by immersion; leaders called of God; sealings on earth and in heaven; baptism for the dead.

In our church, we have the same offices and teachings as Jesus did. This is how we know our church is organized correctly. Both churches—in Jesus' time and now—are the same. The Lord added to our church's name the phrase "of Latter-day Saints" to show one was in Christ's time and one is now.

I am thankful to know that this is Christ's church, The Church of Jesus Christ of Latter-day Saints, the true church.

Priesthood

The priesthood is the power to act in God's name. In John 15:16, the Lord said: "Ye have not chosen me, but I have chosen you, and ordained you." God chooses whom he wants to hold the priesthood.

With the priesthood, our fathers and older brothers can do special things. They can heal and bless the sick, give names and blessings to new babies, give father's blessings, baptize, and give the gift of the Holy Ghost. We are blessed to have the priesthood and its power in our homes.

43

Primary

 I am a Sunbeam.
I can come to Primary every Sunday.

 I learn stories about Jesus.

 I learn new songs to sing.

 I make new friends.

 I love to come to Primary.

Revelation

The ninth article of faith reads: "We believe all that God has revealed, all that He does now reveal, and we believe that He will yet reveal many great and important things pertaining to the Kingdom of God."

We are blessed to have revelation. Revelation comes when God speaks to man.

The Church was restored to earth by revelation. The priesthood and sacrament prayers were given by revelation. The baptismal prayers were revealed, and so were the temple ordinances.

We have had special revelations recently. All worthy male members of the Church hold the priesthood now, new editions of the scriptures have been published, and new temple locations have been announced. All are revelations in the latter days.

God will continue to speak to the prophet, guiding and helping us to prepare for Christ's second coming. I hope we will accept the new revelations that come and be thankful for them.

Sunday

One of the Ten Commandments is: "Remember the sabbath day, to keep it holy" (Exodus 20:8). Sunday is the Sabbath day. It is a day to remember the Lord. We should not work on Sunday. When the world was created it took six days, and on the seventh day the Lord rested. He told us we should also rest on the seventh day, the Sabbath day.

We can do many things on Sunday. We can go to church, write in our journals, visit our grandparents, visit sick people, write letters to missionaries, or prepare a lesson for family night.

Sunday is a special day. We should feel good about it. We should remember it is the Lord's day.

45

Temples

A temple is a very special place. It is the house of God. God tells the prophet where and when to build temples.

Temples are used for sacred things. In temples couples can be married for time and all eternity, making important promises to the Lord. Work for the dead—such as baptism—is done in temples. Special prayers are given for those in need. Joseph Smith prayed when he dedicated the Kirtland temple that the temple would "be a house of prayer, a house of fasting, a house of faith, a house of glory and of God, even thy house" (D&C 109:16).

Our prophet has told us to have a picture of a temple in our bedrooms so we can look at it every day. All of us should want to be married in the temple and live so we can go there to do God's work.

Tithing

We should all pay our tithing. It is a commandment from God. God gives us everything we have. He asks us to pay ten percent to the Church in tithing. Ten percent is one out of ten. If we have ten pennies, one goes to tithing.

The bishop has an envelope for us to put our tithing in. (Show an envelope.)

Every year in December we go to tithing settlement. We tell the bishop if we have paid a full tithing—ten percent of all the money we earn or are given each year.

I hope we will all pay our tithing. We will be blessed if we do. God said that if we pay our tithing, he would "open the windows of heaven, and pour [us] out a blessing that there shall not be room enough to receive it" (Malachi 3:10).

We Must Prepare

President Kimball has told us to be prepared in six areas. This is for our families and for us as individuals. I would like to tell you about these areas and what we can do to prepare.

Education. We should learn all kinds of things, everything from how to read good books to how to use the dishwasher.

Career Development. We should learn to work and enjoy working. We should always finish what we start.

Financial. We should pay our tithing and always save some of what we earn.

Home Production. We can help plant a garden and weed it.

Physical. We should eat good foods, go to bed early, and exercise.

Social and Spiritual. We can read the scriptures, go to church, and have family night.

We should help our families get prepared in these six different areas.

When I Pray

When I pray, I talk to my Heavenly Father. I should say my prayers in the morning when I get up and at night when I go to bed. I should pray before I eat, thanking the Lord for the food and asking him to bless it. I should pray with my family in family prayer. I should pray when I need help.

I can pray anywhere, but it is good to pray in a quiet place where I can bow my head, fold my arms, and close my eyes.

I hope we will always remember to pray.

Work

Have you ever thought of work as a blessing? It is, and it is very necessary.

Adam, the first man on earth, was told he had to work. In Genesis 3:19, God said: "In the sweat of thy face shalt thou eat bread."

There are at least two kinds of work. We can work to provide our food, clothes, and other daily needs. We can also work to build up the Church.

We should remember some things about work. We should have a good attitude about it. We should work without complaining. We should do our jobs the best we can. We should finish every job we start. We should try to help others with their work.

I hope we will all try to look at work differently, doing it willingly and with a cheerful heart. We should be glad we can work.

3

First Principles

Baptism

When we turn eight years old, we will be baptized. When we are baptized and confirmed, we become members of The Church of Jesus Christ of Latter-day Saints. The scriptures tell us how we should be baptized. We should be baptized the same way Jesus was.

Matthew 3:16 reads: "And Jesus, when he was baptized, went up straightway out of the water." Like Jesus, we must go completely under the water and come straight out of it. If a hand or a toe does not go under the water, we must be baptized again. The prayer for baptism is found in the Doctrine and Covenants. It must be said exactly by one having priesthood authority to do it.

Baptism is a special ordinance. It will make us members of the Church. We should all look forward to being baptized.

Faith

We are told to have faith, but what is faith? Faith means to believe in something even though we cannot see it.

When we look at a seed and plant it in the ground, we believe it will grow; that is faith. Alma 32:21 says: "therefore if ye have faith ye hope for things which are not seen, which are true."

We have faith in God and Jesus even though we don't see them. The more we believe, or have faith, the more God blesses us and helps our faith grow. We pray to God because of our faith; our prayers are answered so our faith grows. It goes on and on.

I hope we will all develop our faith.

Faith to Be Healed

There was a woman who was very ill. She believed Jesus could make her well. She tried to get to Jesus. She worked her way through the crowds. Her faith was so great that she was healed just by touching Jesus' clothes.

People heard of Jesus' miracles. People believed they could be healed just by touching Jesus' clothes. In the city of Gennesaret, all who did this were healed.

When we are sick, we can be administered to by someone holding the priesthood. If we have faith, we can also be made well.

People showed faith by touching Christ's clothes. We show faith by asking for priesthood blessings.

We are blessed to have the priesthood available to bless us.

The Holy Ghost

The first article of faith is: "We believe in God, the Eternal Father, and in His Son, Jesus Christ, and in the Holy Ghost."

The Holy Ghost is the third member of the Godhead. He does not have a body of flesh and bones; he has only a spirit.

He helps Heavenly Father and Jesus. He tells us things they want us to know. He will help us make right choices. He can warn us of danger. He testifies of Christ.

When we are baptized we get the gift of the Holy Ghost. That means if we are worthy he will stay with us.

I hope we will obey the commandments so the Holy Ghost will be with us to help us.

Jesus' Atonement

The third article of faith says: "We believe that through the Atonement of Christ, all mankind may be saved, by obedience to the laws and ordinances of the Gospel."

When Jesus suffered in the garden and on the cross, he did it for us. He took upon himself the sins of *all* the world. He died and was resurrected so we could be forgiven of our sins. He made it possible to overcome both physical and spiritual death.

Jesus did his part, but we must do ours, too. We must repent. We must change and be obedient for Jesus' atonement to help us. If we don't repent, then someday we will have to be punished for our sins. We must repent, be baptized, and obey the laws.

Jesus tried to help us; he gave up his life for us. I hope we will do our part so his suffering will not have been done in vain.

Keep the Commandments

"If ye love me, keep my commandments" (John 14:15). Even children can keep the commandments:

We can pay tithing.
We can obey our mothers and fathers.
We can go to church on Sunday.
We can be kind to others.

We should all show Jesus that we love him by keeping his commandments.

Love

Jesus said, "Love one another, as I have loved you" (John 15:12). In Primary, we sing a song that uses this scripture. It tells us that we should love everyone.

We can show our love for others by our actions. We should not quarrel or fight. We should be kind and help other people. We should be polite, always saying "please" and "thank you." We should try to be friends with everyone at school, at home, and at church. We should try to help people without being asked.

Showing our love to others is like showing our love to Jesus. Doctrine and Covenants 42:38 reads: "For inasmuch as ye do it unto the least of these, ye do it unto me."

Obedience

"Not every one that saith unto me, Lord, Lord, shall enter into the kingdom of heaven; but he that doeth the will of my Father which is in heaven" (Matthew 7:21). We cannot just talk about our love for Jesus and his church. We cannot just say that we want to do what is right. We should do what he asks and show by our actions that we love him. We must be obedient to his commandments.

We should be obedient to Church laws, to family rules, and to city and government laws. Since actions speak louder than words, we must show by our actions that we will obey all the laws. Then we can enter into our Heavenly Father's kingdom.

Prayer

Matthew 21:22 reads: "And all things, whatsoever ye shall ask in prayer, believing, ye shall receive." Prayer is very important. When we pray, we talk to our Heavenly Father. Prayer is like a long-distance phone call. God is always there to listen, but we must do the calling. He wants to know how we are, what we are thankful for, and what we need.

Just as we talk to our earthly parents, God wants us to talk to him. We should not say the same prayer all the time or use the same words. We should begin our prayers in his name and close in the name of Jesus Christ.

I hope we will all say our prayers, remembering that when we pray we talk to our Heavenly Father.

Purpose of Life

We came to earth for at least two reasons: to get a body and to prove that we can obey the Lord's commandments.

The Lord said: "This life is the time for men to prepare to meet God; yea, behold the day of this life is the day for men to perform their labors" (Alma 34:32). This scripture tells us that we must prove ourselves now. We must show the Lord that we can do what is right. We cannot just say that we want to live with God again, we must show that we want to—today and every day. By obeying God's laws, we can show that we are worthy to live with him again.

Repentance

In Doctrine and Covenants 19:4, the Lord said: "And surely every man must repent." None of us are perfect. We all make mistakes. That is why we all need to repent. Repentance has four steps:

First:　　We must feel sorry for the wrong we did.

Second:　We should tell the Lord in prayer what we did—confess our sins. If our wrong hurt anyone else, we should also apologize to that person.

Third:　　We must make up for what we did wrong. For example, if we took something that was not ours, we must return it.

Fourth:　We must do what is right and not do the wrong again.

In Doctrine and Covenants 58:42, God said: "Behold, he who has repented of his sins, the same is forgiven, and I, the Lord, remember them no more."

If we repent, the Lord forgives us, and he forgets our sins. Repentance is like erasing the sin. To be forgiven, all we need to do is to repent.

The Sacrament

Every Sunday when we go to sacrament meeting we take the sacrament. We do this to remember Jesus. Jesus said: "This [the sacrament] is my body which is given for you: this do in remembrance of me" (Luke 22:19).

When the sacrament prayers are said, we should listen to the words. After we are baptized, each time we take the sacrament we will renew our baptismal covenants—the promises we make to the Lord. When the sacrament is being passed, we should sit quietly and think about Jesus. We could think about his life, his teachings, and his miracles. Jesus died for us so we can repent, be forgiven of our sins, and live with him some day.

Taking the bread and water of the sacrament is the most important thing we do on Sunday.

Testimony

I am a child of God. I am very lucky to know this. Some people don't know about God, or Jesus, or their church. So as a member of Christ's church, I have a special mission. I must tell people about Jesus and his church. I must prepare them for when he comes again. I can do this by bearing my testimony to them.

When I bear my testimony, I should say that I believe Jesus is the Son of God, that Joseph Smith was a prophet, and that our church is the true church.

If you want a testimony you should pray for one, study the scriptures, and obey the commandments. Moroni wrote: "And by the power of the Holy Ghost ye may know the truth of all things" (Moroni 10:5).

I hope we will all try to gain a testimony.

4

Home and Family

Children Should Honor Their Parents

One of the Ten Commandments is to honor our fathers and mothers.

Ephesians 6:1 says: "Children, obey your parents in the Lord: for this is right." We can honor our parents in many ways. We can honor them by—

Listening to their advice, and doing what they ask.
Being polite when talking to them or about them.
Remembering them in our prayers.
Trying to help them without being asked.
Telling them we love them.

I hope we will all try harder to honor our parents.

Families

Our families are the most important people on earth. The scriptures tell us that the first family was Adam and Eve. All through the scriptures we learn of families: Noah and his family went on the ark; Moses brought his family and the other children of Israel out of Egypt; Lehi and his family came to the Americas.

In Doctrine and Covenants 88:119, the Lord tells us several steps that a family can apply to their home: "Organize yourselves; prepare every needful thing; and establish a house, even a house of prayer, a house of fasting, a house of faith, a house of learning, a house of glory, a house of order, a house of God."

We should help our families do the things God has told us to do. If we keep the commandments, we can be a family forever.

Family Home Evening

Every Monday night we have family home evening. I like family home evening.

I like to help. We all take turns. Sometimes I say the prayer or lead the song. Sometimes I help Mom fix the refreshments. I can even help give the lesson.

When we have family night, we feel closer as a family. I hope we will all have family home evening.

Genealogy

We sing a song in Primary about genealogy. Genealogy is a record of our relatives, our parents, our grandparents, and great-grandparents.

We can put all these records and information in a book. This book is called a "book of remembrance."

A book of remembrance should have our relatives listed on a family tree. It should have our personal history and pictures. We should put special experiences and certificates in it.

Even people in olden times kept books of remembrance. Moses 6:46 says: "For a book of remembrance we have written among us, according to the pattern given by the finger of God."

We should go home and ask our parents to help us start our own book of remembrance.

Home

President David O. McKay said: "Home can be a bit of heaven on earth."

We can all help to make our homes nice places. We can smile and be happy. We can say "please" and "thank you." We can share our toys and put them away when we are through playing with them. We can do our jobs without complaining. We can try never to argue or fight.

I hope we will all try to make our homes a bit of heaven on earth.

63

I Am Glad to Be Me

I am thankful for my eyes. I can see the beautiful sunset at night. I can see the butterflies and the birds. I can see green trees blowing in the wind and the tiny snowflakes as they fall from the sky.

I am thankful for my ears. I can hear my mom singing a lullaby and my dad whistling as he works. I can hear the cat's meow and the bird's song. I can hear the prayer when someone is baptized and the Tabernacle Choir singing at general conference.

I am thankful for my nose; I can smell the flowers and fresh baked bread.

I am thankful for lips to sing songs of praise and tell Heavenly Father "thank you."

I am glad to be me.

Keep a Journal

The prophet has told us we should keep a journal. Everyone in the Church should.

In our journals, we can write many things: the day, month, and year; what we did that day; how we felt; what we learned; and what happened.

When Nephi started to write a journal, he wrote: "And I know that the record which I make is true; and I make it with mine own hand; and I make it according to my knowledge" (1 Nephi 1:30). We know about Nephi and his people because he kept a record. We know about the pioneers because some of them kept journals and wrote about their experiences. We need to keep a journal to tell other people about us.

But the most important thing about keeping a journal is that it shows we are obedient. The Lord told us to do it through our prophet, and we should do it.

"When I'm Helping I'm Happy"

In Primary we sing the song "When I'm Helping I'm Happy." This song's message is true. We can do a lot of things to help at home, and when we help we will be happy. We can—

Set the table.
Put toys away.
Water plants.
Play with younger brothers and sisters.
Make beds.

Helping without being asked makes me feel good inside. I hope we will all help at home.

5

Special People and Special Occasions

America

America is a very special land. It is a land of promise. According to the Book of Mormon, "behold, this is a choice land, and whatsoever nation shall possess it shall be free from bondage . . . if they will but serve the God of the land, who is Jesus Christ" (Ether 2:12).

The Lord brought the Jaredites and the Nephites here to America. Both were destroyed because of wickedness.

Then God brought Columbus to this land. He also guided the Pilgrims here and inspired those who set up our government. The Doctrine and Covenants tells us that our constitution was written by men born for that purpose.

The eleventh article of faith says: "We claim the privilege of worshiping Almighty God according to the dictates of our own conscience, and allow all men the same privilege, let them worship how, where, or what they may."

Heavenly Father wanted America to be a land where we would have religious freedom, where everyone could worship as he wanted.

We should be thankful we live in America, the land of the free.

The Bishop

The bishop of our ward is very special. He was called of God by inspiration to lead the people here. We see him every Sunday sitting on the stand. But do we know what else he does? He does many things.

The Doctrine and Covenants tells the duties of a bishop and says they are given by commandment. That means the Lord tells him what to do. He should use his time to teach and help the people in his ward. He gives food and clothing and money to the poor. He pays the bills for the ward. He meets with priesthood holders and teaches them.

The bishop is busy and has a lot to do. We can help him by doing what he asks us to do. This will make our bishop and our Father in Heaven happy.

Brigham Young, Our Second President

When Joseph Smith was killed, the Church was without a President. The members did not know who should be the next President. Sidney Rigdon thought it should be him, but others disagreed.

The members of the Church held a special meeting. All of the Apostles were there. When Brigham Young was speaking, something very special happened. The Holy Ghost came on him, and he changed. His voice sounded like Joseph Smith's, and he looked like Joseph Smith. The people were amazed. They knew that was the Lord's way of telling them who was to be the prophet and President of his church. Brigham Young was made second president of the Church.

The Lord will always watch over and direct his church. Just as he called Joseph Smith and Brigham Young to lead the Church in those days, he chose our current president to lead the Church now.

The fifth article of faith says: "We believe that a man must be called of God, by prophecy, and by the laying on of hands, by those who are in authority to preach the Gospel and administer in the ordinances thereof."

Christmas Gifts

Christmas is to celebrate the birth of Christ, and we should remember all the gifts given at that time.

The sky gave its brightest star. The angels gave their most beautiful chorus. The wise men gave gold, frankincense, and myrrh.

But the most prized gift was that of the Father. The Lord gave his son. John 3:16 says: "For God so loved the world, that he gave his only begotten Son, that whosoever believeth in him should not perish, but have everlasting life."

This Christmas, when we think of giving presents, we should think of God's gift—Jesus Christ.

December

In December we celebrate the birthdays of Joseph Smith and Jesus Christ. They were alike in many ways. Both had special missions. Both taught the gospel plan. Both were very righteous. Both were directed by our Father in Heaven.

We should try to follow their examples and do what is right.

Friends

In the New Testament is a story about a sick man. He could not move his arms or legs. He wanted to see Jesus so he could be made well. But there were always too many people around Jesus.

This man had some very special friends. They loved their friend and wanted to help him. Jesus was in a house with a straw roof. The friends cut a hole in the roof and lowered the sick man down through the hole on a stretcher. Jesus saw the man and made him well so that he could walk.

We should try to be good friends. We should think of ways to help our friends.

Grandma and Grandpa

I am very lucky. I have two special friends. They always love me and the things I do. They always have time for me; they're never too busy.

Who are these friends? They are my grandma and grandpa. I love them, and they love me. Grandma reads me stories and bakes yummy bread. Grandpa takes me on long walks and plays games with me.

I love my family; I am glad Heavenly Father let me have such special grandparents.

Father's Day

F—is the *faith* my father has in his Heavenly Father.
A—means he is *always* there when I need him.
T—stands for *truth*. He never lies.
H—stands for *happy*. We have a good time together.
E—means *everyone* in our family is important to him.
R—means *really*. He is really nice, really special, really great.

I am glad to have a day to honor our fathers.

Jesus

When I go to church, I learn about Jesus. The scriptures tell us of Jesus so we can know more about him. Some of the things I have learned about Jesus are that—

He died for us.
He keeps his promises.
He was baptized.
He obeys Heavenly Father.
He healed the sick.

Nephi wrote: "The words of Christ will tell you all things what ye should do" (2 Nephi 32:3). I know Jesus loves me, and I hope we can learn more about him so we will know what we should do.

Joseph Smith

When Joseph Smith was only fourteen years old, he read a special scripture. It said: "If any of you lack wisdom, let him ask of God . . . and it shall be given him" (James 1:5). Joseph wanted to know what church was true. So he prayed and asked God what church he should join. The Lord told him not to join any of them. None of the churches was true. Through Joseph Smith, God later restored his church, The Church of Jesus Christ of Latter-day Saints. It is the only true church on the earth. I am glad we can become full members of the true church when we turn eight years old.

Lost Lambs

Jesus talked about the shepherd and how he would leave a flock of sheep to find one little lost lamb.

It is the same in our Primary class. Jesus is the shepherd, and we are his sheep. If one of the boys or girls in our class doesn't come, we feel sad. Jesus feels sad. He wants all of us to come to Primary.

I hope we can all help Jesus. We should invite our friends to come with us. We should offer our friends a ride. We could invite a family to our home for family night and talk about how important Primary is.

Let's help Jesus get all his sheep in his fold. Let's get all the boys and girls to Primary.

Lucy Mack Smith

Lucy Mack Smith was Joseph Smith's mother. She helped Joseph and gave him support.

Once Joseph and his brother Hyrum had been administering to the sick. After a while, they both got sick and were afraid they were going to die. As they were praying, Hyrum saw a vision of their mother, Lucy, praying to the Lord to save her sons. Joseph said that he had been saved from death many times because of his mother's prayers.

Lucy was a special woman. We should try to be like her and pray for others.

Mother's Day

My mother is many things. She is a nurse when I am sick. She is a gardener and a teacher. She cooks and sews and washes and irons. She teaches me the gospel. She works a lot and is very busy. But the best thing she does is love me. When she puts a bandage on my hurt knee or tucks me in bed at night, her love makes me feel good inside.

Part of one of the Ten Commandments is to "Honour . . . thy mother" (Exodus 20:12). I am glad Heavenly Father gave me the best mother in the world, and I will love her and honor her all my life.

A New Baby

I have a special family. We all love each other. We have fun together.

Something extra special just happened. We have a new baby at our house. I am so happy. She is so tiny and cute. Now we have even more love in our home. She just came from heaven. We all lived with Heavenly Father before we were born.

I'm glad God gave me such a good family and especially such a sweet baby.

75

Patriotism

We should be proud of the country we live in. We can show that we love our country in many ways:

We can obey the laws.
We can pick up litter when we see it and not be litterbugs.
We can remind our parents to vote.
We can go to town activities.
We can fly our country's flag.

The twelfth article of faith is: "We believe in being subject to kings, presidents, rulers, and magistrates, in obeying, honoring, and sustaining the law."

We should all try to be patriotic citizens.

Pioneers

The pioneers were very brave. They left their homes to come west. God told them to come and told Brigham Young where to lead them.

They went through many hardships. Many died. But they had faith in their Heavenly Father. They knew he was watching over them. God told them: "I am he who led the children of Israel out of the land of Egypt; and my arm is stretched out in the last days, to save my people Israel" (D&C 136:22).

The pioneers walked miles and miles every day. They slept on the ground. They cooked outside and washed their clothes in the river. At night they sang songs and danced around the campfire. They showed the Lord they were a happy and obedient people.

We have different hardships and problems than the pioneers, but we should remember how they accepted theirs and have faith in our Heavenly Father.

A Prophet

A prophet is a man called by God to speak for him. God said: "Whether by mine own voice or by the voice of my servants, it is the same" (D&C 1:38).

The Lord tells his prophet what to do and say, and the prophet tells the people. This is called revelation. Some churches think prophets were only on the earth when the Bible was written. This is not true. We have a prophet today at the head of the Church. He tells us what the Lord tells him. All the presidents of our church were prophets. Joseph Smith was the first prophet in our time.

We should thank our Heavenly Father for the prophet and ask Him to bless him. When the prophet tells us what to do, it is the Lord's will. We should do it.

Rainbows and Dads

When I see a rainbow it reminds me that Heavenly Father loves me and is watching over me. Our fathers also love us and watch over us. They help us here on earth and remind us of our Heavenly Father's love.

Even the colors in the rainbow remind me of my dad:

Purple is for Royalty. My dad is a son of God.
Blue is for purity in both thought and deed.
Green is for life. We should try to live so we can be a family forever.
Red is for courage. My dad always does what is right.
Orange reminds me of a warm fire. My dad's smile makes me feel warm inside.
Yellow is like the sunshine. My dad brightens my day and makes me happy.

Sometimes when things go wrong it is like a rainy, stormy day, but my dad can change things so I feel happy and everything is better. He really brightens up my life.

I am thankful that God made rainbows and dads.

Resurrection

When we celebrate Easter, we think of Christ's crucifixion and resurrection in Judea. How many times do we think about what happened in America? After Christ was resurrected, he came to the Americas.

In 3 Nephi 11:7, the Book of Mormon tells us that the people in America heard a voice from heaven saying: "Behold my Beloved Son, in whom I am well pleased." They saw Jesus coming from the heavens dressed in white. He taught the people. He baptized them and called twelve disciples. He blessed and healed the sick. He gave the people the sacrament. When he was about to leave, he had the little children gather around him and he blessed them. Angels came from heaven and ministered to the children.

When we think of Christ this Easter, we should remember what he did when he came to America.

Thanksgiving

On Thanksgiving:

T—is for *thanks.* We should pray and give thanks for all we have.

H—is for the *homes* we live in and need to be thankful for.

A—is for *all* we have, for all of our blessings.

N—is for the *nuts* in the forest for the Pilgrims.

K—is for the *kernels* of corn the Pilgrims planted.

S—is for our *songs* of praise.

G—is for *God* who gave us all we have.

I—is for the *Indians* who taught the Pilgrims how to live on this land.

V—is for the *variety* of fruits and vegetables the earth produces.

I—is for the *inspiration* Columbus received to sail his ships to America.

N—is for *November,* the month in which we celebrate the harvest.

G—is for the *gospel* which blesses our lives.

This is what Thanksgiving means to me.

Women in Church History

In our Church history we find some very special women. I would like to tell you about some of them.

Emma Smith was the wife of Joseph Smith. She made a collection of hymns for the first Church hymnbook. She was in charge of the first Relief Society. Sometimes she served as scribe while Joseph translated the golden plates.

Aurelia S. Rogers was another special lady. She was the first Primary president and held the first meeting on 25 August 1878.

Lucy Mack Smith was the mother of Joseph Smith. She helped hide the golden plates so they would not be stolen.

Women in Church history have played a very important part. They have set a good example for us.

6

Personal Qualities

Anger

Anger is a feeling that we need to learn to control. Proverbs 16:32 says: "He that is slow to anger is better than the mighty."

Heavenly Father does not want us to get angry or upset. Anger can hurt us. It is hard to think or reason when we are mad. Anger can ruin friendships. Sometimes we say things we do not mean and hurt other people's feelings. Anger is the spirit of the devil.

There are ways to control our anger. Some of these ways are to go for a walk, sing a song, weed the garden, jump rope, or pray. If we do not feel like praying, we should stay on our knees until we do. We should ask for the Spirit of the Lord to help us.

I hope we will all try to control our anger.

Cleanliness

Doctrine and Covenants 42:41 reads: "And let all things be done in cleanliness before me."

Heavenly Father has told us many times in the scriptures to be clean. We should be clean in our thoughts and words. We should keep our bodies clean.

We should also keep our homes clean. That means we should help Mother sweep the floor, dust, vacuum, wash the windows, and polish the furniture. Picking up our toys and dirty clothes helps keep our homes clean, too.

We are told to keep our yards clean. We should pull the weeds, paint the fences, and fix up what is broken.

Everyone in the family should help. I hope we can all help keep our homes clean inside and out.

Courage

We can look to people in the Church for examples in our lives. When we learn how they act, we will know how we should act. It helps us to know other people have gone through similar experiences.

Joseph Smith is a great example to me in many ways. All the stories I hear about him help me to pattern my life.

The last time he was put in jail the guards were using bad language and telling bad stories. They boasted of how they robbed and killed the Saints. They told of how they hurt women and children. They laughed loudly and bragged all night. Finally, Joseph could stand it no longer. Even though he was in chains, he stood with power and commanded the guards to be quiet. They obeyed. They told Joseph they were sorry.

Joseph knew that he had to stand for the right. We should have the same courage to defend the right, no matter what.

Example

Matthew 5:14 reads: "Ye are the light of the world. A city that is set on an hill cannot be hid." This scripture means that members of Christ's church are examples to others. People look up to us just as they might look up to a city on a hill.

Because of this, we should set a good example in everything we do and say. We should always be honest, respect our parents, and do what is right. Many people think that if they see a Latter-day Saint do something it must be all right. If we cannot decide whether something is right or wrong, we should ask ourselves: "What would Jesus do?" Then we should do what he would do.

Many people—even our younger brothers and sisters —watch the examples we set. I hope we can all be good examples.

Forgiveness

In Doctrine and Covenants 64:9, God says: "Wherefore, I say unto you, that ye ought to forgive one another." Forgiveness is part of repentance. We can be forgiven, but we must also forgive others. If we really forgive someone, we will forget what he did and never talk about it. It is as though it never happened.

Jesus showed the best example of forgiveness when he was on the cross and said this about the people who crucified him: "Father, forgive them; for they know not what they do" (Luke 23:34).

Like Jesus, we should all try to forgive others. If we learn to forgive when we are young, it will be easier when we grow up.

Give a Gift

Acts 20:35 reads: "Remember the words of the Lord Jesus, how he said, It is more blessed to give than to receive."

We can give many things to others every day. Give a smile. Give a friendly "hello." Give time—do a job for someone; tend a child; read a story to someone. Give the gift of music—sing a song to someone. Give the gift of love—give someone a hug and a kiss. Give the gospel—invite someone over for family night.

When we give to others, it makes us feel good inside. I hope we will give a gift to someone today.

Hands

Doctrine and Covenants 42:40 talks about worldly riches and teaches that the beauty of our clothes should be "the beauty of the work of [our] own hands."

The Lord is pleased when we work with our hands. We should develop those talents that God has given us. We should appreciate handmade items.

There are many kinds of things our hands can do. We can sew, make bread, paint, sculpture, draw, or play the piano. Some people can even talk with their hands by using sign language.

I am glad Heavenly Father gave me hands.

Happiness

2 Nephi 2:25 says: "Men are, that they might have joy."

Jesus wants us to be happy. He wants us to love life, to wake up in the morning with a smile. If we share our happiness and smiles with those we meet, there will be more love and kindness and joy in the world.

The best way to be happy is to obey the commandments. If we do something wrong we are unhappy. If we keep the commandments we feel good inside. God knew how to make us happy and that is why he gave us the commandments.

I hope we will try to be more happy by keeping the commandments. I hope we will also share our happiness by smiling at others.

Honesty

In Romans 13:13, the Apostle Paul wrote: "Let us walk honestly, as in the day." We should be honest in everything we do, as if we were in front of other people in the light of day. We should always tell the truth and not lie. We should keep the promises we make. We should pay our tithing—a full ten percent. We should not take anything that is not ours. "Finders keepers, losers weepers" is not right. If we find something we should try to return it. We should not cheat on tests in school; that is like stealing —stealing an answer that is not ours.

The thirteenth article of faith says, "We believe in being honest." I hope we will all be honest in everything we do.

Knowledge

It is important that we study, learn, and gain knowledge. What we learn will remain with us when we are resurrected. We should learn about God and his laws. Doctrine and Covenants 131:6 reads: "It is impossible for a man to be saved in ignorance." Just because we do not know the law is no excuse to do wrong acts. It is our responsibility and duty to learn the laws. The Lord will help us. The Holy Ghost will help us.

The more we learn, the more we will understand about God. If we want to become like him, we must know what he knows. One way we can do this is to study. This could include reading the scriptures; listening to general conference; reading the *Ensign, New Era,* and *Friend*; attending Sunday meetings; listening to our teachers and parents; and having family home evenings.

I hope we will all study to learn more about God and his ways so that we can become like him.

Listening

Jesus told us in Mark 4:23: "If any man have ears to hear, let him hear." We all need to learn to listen. We talk and sing and cry and laugh. All these are necessary. But sometimes we need to listen—just be quiet and listen, listen for the still small voice.

After we say our prayers we should stay on our knees and listen. We should ask for help and then we should listen for the answer.

We wouldn't call someone on the phone, ask a question, and then hang up before we hear an answer. It's the same with prayer. We call on the Lord and ask for his help. We should also learn to *listen* to the answer.

If the answer is yes, we will feel good inside. If the answer is no, we will feel confused and uncomfortable.

Another time we should listen is when we talk to our father and mother. We should let them explain themselves and tell how they feel.

I hope we will spend more time listening and less time talking—at home, at school, and when we pray. We *need* to listen.

Peace

Jesus taught us that peace is very important. Matthew 5:9 reads: "Blessed are the peacemakers: for they shall be called the children of God."

We should try to be peacemakers at home, at school, and at play. We should try to get along with others. We should not fight or argue. If someone hurts us, we should turn the other cheek; in other words, we should forgive him and try to be friends. We should use kind words and be polite. We should share all that we have. We should remember in our prayers to ask for more peace at home and in the world. The spirit of fighting is of the devil; the spirit of peace is of Christ.

We sometimes sing the words, "Let there be peace on earth, and let it begin with me." I hope we will do our parts to let peace begin with each one of us.

Reverence

When we go to church we should be reverent. What does it mean to be reverent? It means we should sit quietly. We should not play or talk loudly. We should not run through the building, because it is the Lord's house. But being reverent is more than that. We should think about the stories in the scriptures. We should listen to the prayers that are said and the music that is played. We should be on time so we do not interrupt the meeting. We should be reverent outside as well as inside the church. Our minds should be reverent. The Lord said: "Be still, and know that I am God" (Psalm 46:10).

If we sit quietly and think about why we are in church, we can feel closer to our Heavenly Father.

Service

In Primary, we sing the song "Jesus Wants Me for a Sunbeam." Even the littlest children know this song. It is about service.

Jesus taught a lot about service. He taught the Golden Rule: "As ye would that men should do to you, do ye also to them likewise" (Luke 6:31). He said that we should go the second mile and do more than we are asked to do. He said that we should help the sick, the poor, and the needy.

In the Church we can serve all the time. Whenever Church leaders ask us to do something we should do it. We should be like Joshua when he said: "As for me and my house, we will serve the Lord" (Joshua 24:15).

I hope we will all be sunbeams for Jesus, serving other people and the Lord.

Speak No Evil

James 4:11 reads: "Speak not evil one of another."

This means we shouldn't say bad things about someone else. If someone tries to tell us about another person, we should not listen.

Ecclesiastes 3:7 says that there is "a time to keep silence, and a time to speak." I hope we will all learn how to keep silent and not spread gossip.

Spiritual Gifts

The Holy Ghost gives each of us special gifts. We should share our spiritual gifts with each other.

One gift is that of testimony—to know Jesus is the Son of God. Another gift is that of leadership—the ability to direct others.

There also is the gift of faith to be healed, the gift to know good and evil spirits, the gift to teach, and the gift to speak or understand a strange language.

The seventh article of faith says: "We believe in the gift of tongues, prophecy, revelation, visions, healing, interpretation of tongues, etc."

We should learn the gifts we have and then use them to bless others.

Talents

The Lord has given all of us talents. Some people can sing; some can draw; some can run very fast; some are always happy and have pretty smiles; some have the ability to make friends. Everyone is blessed with talents of one kind or another.

We are told to improve our talents. We should practice and share them with others. In Doctrine and Covenants 82:18, the Lord said: "Every man may improve upon his talent, that every man may gain other talents." If we want more talents we must first use the ones we have.

If you do not think you have a talent, ask your parents; they can help you to discover your talent. They can also help it to grow. Asking this would be a good thing to do in family night. I hope we will all try to find and use our talents.

Thankfulness

King Benjamin said: "O how ye ought to thank your heavenly King!" (Mosiah 2:19). We should thank God for many things:

For our families and friends.
For our homes.
For the food we have to eat.
For the animals.
For the beautiful world.
For the Church.

We should thank our Heavenly Father for our blessings when we say our prayers.

95

Truth

Doctrine and Covenants 93:24 reads: "And truth is knowledge of things as they are, and as they were, and as they are to come."

We ought to always tell the truth.

When Joseph Smith was just fifteen years old he went through a lot of persecution. People were mean to him. He didn't understand why. Joseph Smith wrote: "I have actually seen a vision; and who am I that I can withstand God?" (JS—H 2:25). He knew that he had seen God and Jesus. They had talked to him and Joseph could not deny it. Even though eventually he was murdered for it, he spoke the truth.

We should be like Joseph Smith and always tell the truth.

We Should Be Happy

The prophet Lehi said: "Men are, that they might have joy" (2 Nephi 2:25). Our Heavenly Father wants us to be happy. He has given us many things to help us be happy.

For example, he created this beautiful world for us. When we see a pretty sunset, hear the rain fall at night, or smell the clean mountain air, we should be happy we live here.

God also gave us our families to make us happy. Seeing a new baby blessed, having family night, and singing songs around the campfire makes me smile and feel good inside.

Our Heavenly Father wants us to be happy. He wants us to enjoy the blessings he has given us. I hope we will try hard to be happy.